D0568936

A PARRAGON BOOK

Published by Parragon Book Service Ltd,
Units 13-17, Avonbridge Trading Estate,
Atlantic Road, Avonmouth, Bristol BS11 9QD

Produced by The Templar Company plc,
Pippbrook Mill, London Road, Dorking, Surrey RH4 1JE

Copyright © 1996 Parragon Book Service Ltd

Designed by Janie Louise Hunt
Edited by Caroline Repchuk and Dugald Steer

All rights reserved

Printed in Italy

ISBN 0-75251-438-5

Jam Pandas

PICTURE
DICTIONARY

Illustrated by STEPHANIE BOEY

‖ •PARRAGON• ‖

Contents

Colours and Shapes

blue
rectangle

orange
diamond

red square

green oval

brown semi-circle

grey cube

pink cylinder

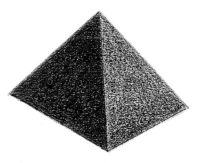

black pyramid

yellow triangle

white star

purple cone

Getting Dressed

coat

shirt

dress

hat

shoes

socks

dungarees

apron

trousers

buttons

belt

shorts

scarf

necklace

pocket

jumper

shoe-laces

jacket

t-shirt

zip

The Body

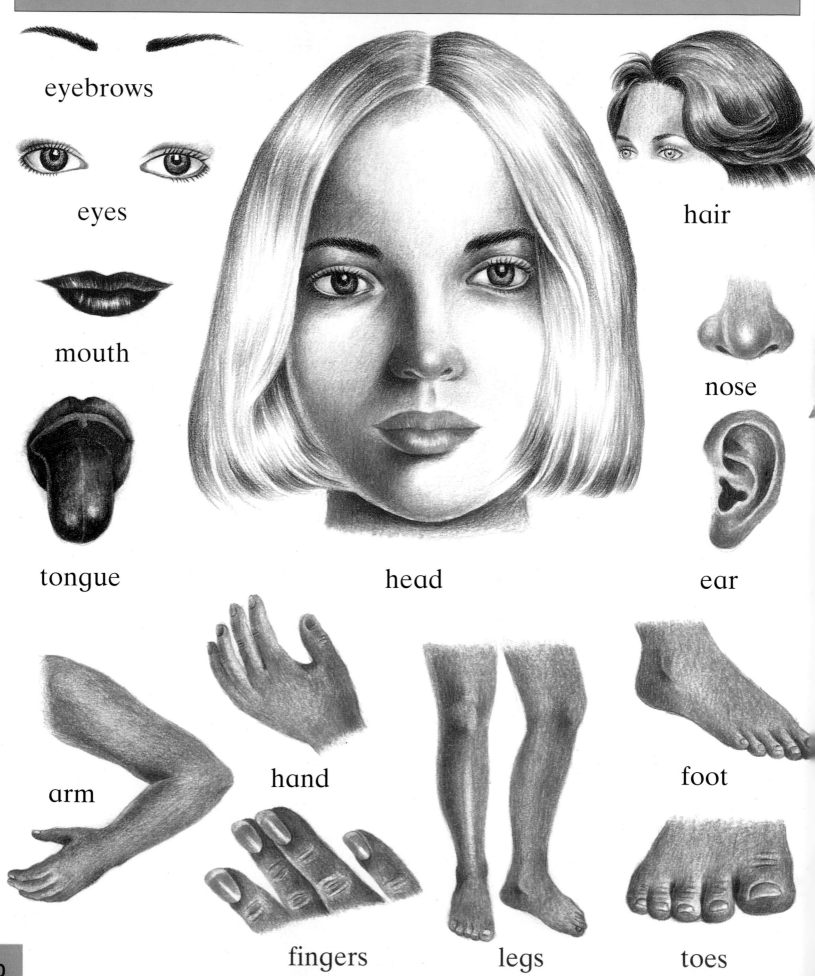

eyebrows

eyes

mouth

tongue

hair

nose

ear

head

arm

hand

foot

fingers

legs

toes

head

eyes

nose

mouth

cheeks

shoulders

neck

arm

hand

waist

fingers

knees

legs

feet

toes

11

Getting About

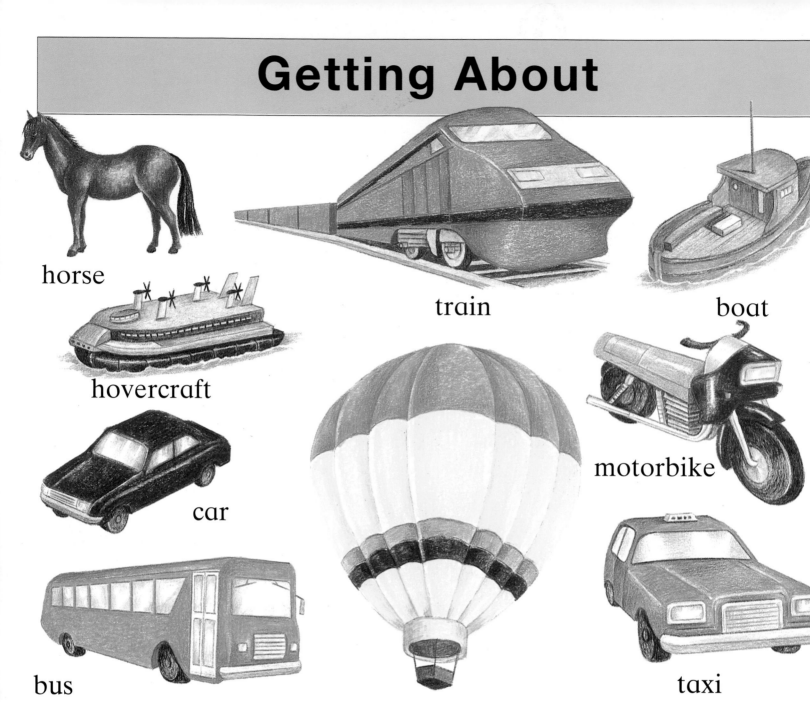

horse

train

boat

hovercraft

motorbike

car

bus

hot-air balloon

taxi

roller-skates

aeroplane

lorry

bicycle

tandem

tricycle

12

At the Airport

helicopter

aeroplane

passengers

check-in desk

landing

14

suitcase

control tower

runway

taking off

air stewardess

pilot

15

At the Station

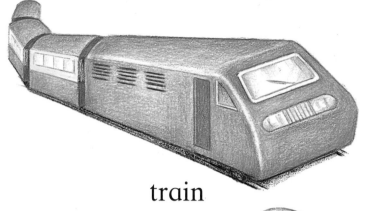
train

guard

passenger

drinks machine

ticket office

driver

seat

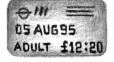
ticket

suitcase

newspaper

porter

magazine

ticket
inspector

holiday-makers

briefcase

news-stand

timetable

rails

At the Garage

mechanic

spanners

workbench

truck

car

van

petrol can

nuts and bolts

hammer

screwdriver

drill

file

dustpan and brush

tool-box

torch

bucket

nails

broom

19

Things We Do

sleeping

dancing

writing

drawing

cooking

singing

reading

eating

crawling

climbing

knitting   shopping   dressing up   swinging

In the Playground

doll

ball

bricks

sandpit

teddy bear

swing

roller-skates

slide

football

skateboard

kite

seesaw

skipping-rope

bicycle

jumping

running

toy train

catching

throwing

At Work

painter

nurse

teacher

carpenter

builder

astronaut

doctor

mechanic

cook

hairdresser

postman

scientist

ambulance man

fireman

dustman

In the Hospital

plaster

nurse

bed

scissors

syringe

grapes

x-ray

wheelchair

bandage

chart

doctor

glass

blanket

26

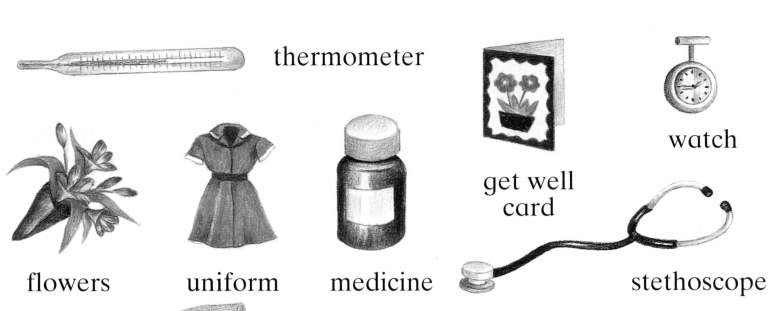

thermometer

flowers   uniform   medicine

get well card

watch

stethoscope

In the Classroom

teacher

scissors

books

student

desk

easel

picture

paper

crayons

ruler

crayons

textbook

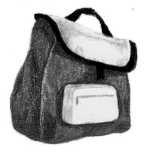

rucksack

shelves

paintbrushes

computer

paint　　　　**models**　　　　**chalk**　　　　　　**map**

Sports Day

running shoes

shorts

headband

vest

stopwatch

hurdles

race track

whistle

flag

silver medal

gold medal

bronze medal

crowd

first

second

third

The High Street

pram

drain

pavement

skateboard

roller-skates

motorbike

bicycle

policeman

lollipop lady

baker

rubbish bin

bus

butcher

car

traffic
lights

33

At the Greengrocer's

apples

pears

bananas

oranges

grapefruit

pineapple

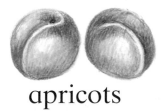
apricots

melon

cherries

plums

blackcurrants

strawberries

lemons

lettuce

cabbage

cauliflower

potatoes

onions

carrots

grapes

peppers

peas

raspberries

tomatoes

beans

courgettes

At the Toy Shop

teddy bear

aeroplane

doll

boat

book

car

jigsaw

clockwork mouse

panda

dominoes

rocket

doll's house

rocking horse

jack-in-the-box

bat

ball

drum

soldier

skipping-rope

building bricks

37

At the Supermarket

doughnuts

trolley

fish

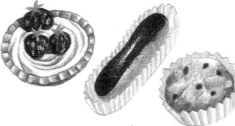
cakes

jam

basket

beans

vegetables

till

cheese

milk

sausages

bread

bacon

apples

eggs

ice
lolly

toilet roll

flour

tomato
ketchup

washing
powder

washing-up
liquid

carrier bag

At the Pet Shop

kitten

budgie

tropical fish

mouse

snake

goldfish

puppy

bone

squeaky toy

birdseed

basket

lead

hamster   rabbit   parrot   cage

A Big Band

drum

cymbals

violin

maracas

trombone

conductor

triangle

xylophone

piano

recorder

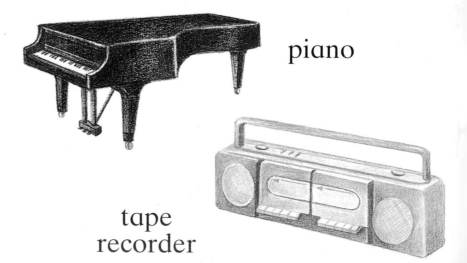
tape recorder

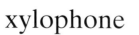

cello   tambourine

trumpet

songbook

flute   saxophone

Party Time

cake

sweets

biscuits

streamers

sandwich

balloon

bow

present

rabbit

magician

fancy dress costume

party hat

card

prizes

candles

jelly

lemonade

hat

magic wand

In the Bathroom

nail-file

tap

sink

bath

shower

bubbles

towel

soap

mirror

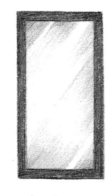

shampoo

toothpaste

toothbrush

bathroom cabinet

comb

toilet

sponge

duck

scales

nail-brush

hairbrush

bath mat

In the Kitchen

oven

oven glove

saucepan

frying pan

apron

plate

cup and saucer

knives

forks

spoons

salt and pepper

48

washing machine

table

clock

broom

sink

teapot

jug

toast rack

toast

jam pots

mixing bowl

In the Living Room

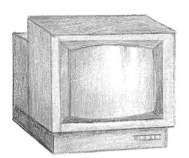

television

rug

vase

picture

magazine

books

piano

sofa

grandfather
clock

photograph

lamp

plant

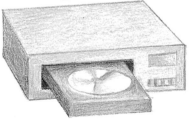

CD player

armchair

fireplace

window

door

In the Nursery

teddy bear

cot

doll

bottle

blanket

nappy

talcum powder

dummy

mobile

toy box

bib

high chair

rattle

ball

books

baby

Humpty Dumpty

In the Bedroom

pillow

pyjamas

curtains

bed

lamp

teddy bear

alarm clock

slippers

hot-water
bottle

dressing gown

wardrobe

chair

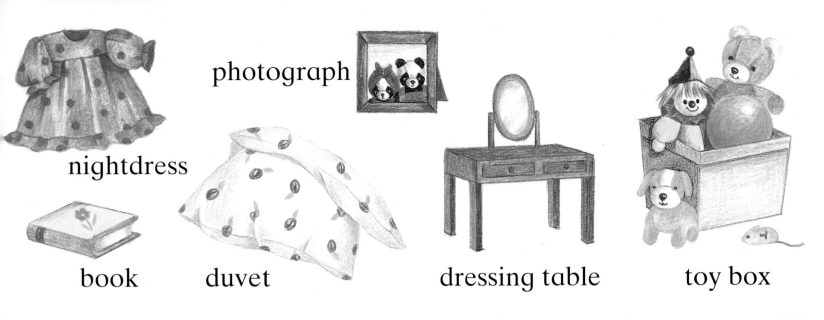

photograph

nightdress

book   duvet   dressing table   toy box

In the Garden

swing

paddling pool

roller

vegetable patch

tree

greenhouse

shed

grass

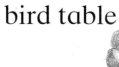

bird table

birdbath

pond

fountain

flowers

compost heap

gnome

wheelbarrow

hose-pipe

trowel

watering can

fork

lawn mower

On the Farm

pig  piglet

sheep  lamb

duck  duckling

chicken  chick

goose  gosling

cow  calf

goat  dog

kid

horse  foal

cat  kitten

puppy

tractor

gate

bucket

farmer

barn

pitchfork

straw

At the Fair

candyfloss

dodgem

ghost train

helter-skelter

ferris wheel

horse

coconut

toy car

raffle ticket

balloons

fortune teller

60

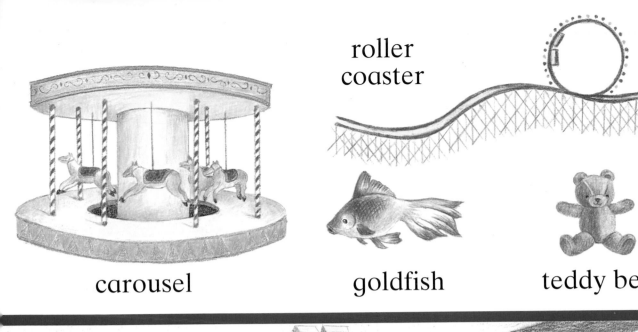

roller
coaster

carousel

goldfish

teddy bear

coconut
shy

At a Pop Concert

drums

keyboard

light

drumsticks

screen

cymbals

stage

microphone

singers

saxophone

loudspeaker

dancer

electric guitar

At the Circus

clown

trapeze artist

lights

horses

acrobat

big top

lion tamer

lion

stilts

ringmaster

ball

elephant

seal

juggler

whip

safety net

At the Zoo

hippo

zebra

monkey

giraffe

snake

rhino

gorilla

penguins

zoo keeper

elephant

tiger

koala

kangaroo

camel

polar bear

parrots

lion

Opposites

tall   short

straight

crooked

open

closed

up

down

fat   thin

push

pull

work

play

over

awake   asleep   under   day   night

69

Feelings

angry

laugh

cry

smile

frown

good

bad

sharing

happy

sad

ill

well

selfish

kind

frightened

71

Weather

windy

calm

dry

wet

hot

cold

rainbow

umbrella

clouds

lightning

rain

sun hat

icicle

sun

puddle

sunglasses

snowflake

73

Springtime

crocus

lamb

duckling

Easter egg

eggs

bird

bird's nest

basket

butterfly

Easter bonnet

tulip

rabbit

daffodil

ribbon

blossom

chicks

hot cross buns

bow

75

By the River

clouds

weeping
willow tree

frog

dragonfly

bridge

water lily

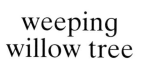

rowing boat

water

fishing rod

fisherman

net

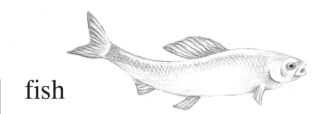

fish

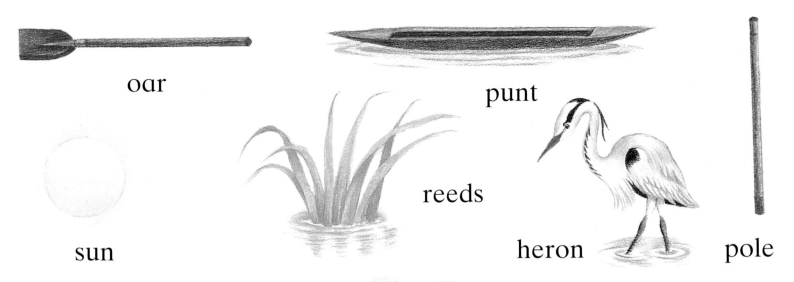

oar

punt

reeds

sun

heron

pole

Summertime

ice lolly

ice cream

strawberries

cream

watermelon

sun

sunflowers

sunshade

juice

hammock

paddling pool

tent

barbecue

grasshopper

deck chair

tennis

At the Seaside

bucket

spade

sand

sandcastle

swimming costume

boat

fishing net

shell

flag

ball

seagull

sun hat

lighthouse

umbrella

sunglasses

crab

starfish

fish

towel

ice cream

At a Picnic

cups

plates

cutlery

paper napkin

blackcurrant juice

jam rolls

jam sandwiches

jam doughnuts

hamper

flask

cow

fruit

rug

kite

Autumn

leaves

harvest festival

fireworks

sparklers

chestnuts

torch

conkers

pumpkin

hot dog

squirrel

bonfire

apples

Halloween

bat

pumpkin

rat

magic wand

cauldron

wizard

magic

pumpkin pie

ghost

witch

broomstick

black cat

spider

web

skeleton

stars

sweets

spell book

moon

monster

Winter

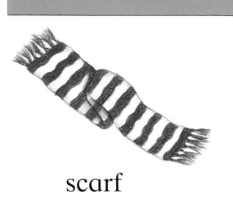

scarf

gloves

hat

ice-skates

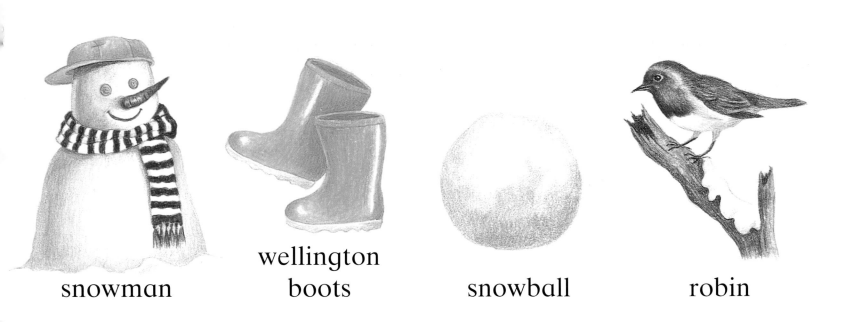

snowman

wellington
boots

snowball

robin

Happy Christmas

cards

holly

mistletoe

fairy

mince pies

Father Christmas

pudding

cake

stocking

crackers

presents

Christmas tree

reindeer

fairy lights

candles

bells

sleigh

Word List